TEAM SPIRIT®

SMART BOOKS FOR YOUNG FANS

THE DETROIT TIGERS

BY
MARK STEWART

NORWOOD HOUSE PRESS
CHICAGO, ILLINOIS

Norwood House Press
P.O. Box 316598
Chicago, Illinois 60631

For information regarding Norwood House Press, please visit our website at:
www.norwoodhousepress.com or call 866-565-2900.

All photos courtesy of Getty Images except the following:
Sweet Caporal (6, 24), Author's Collection (7, 15),
Black Book Partners Archives (10, 11, 23, 25, 31, 33, 35 bottom and top right), 37, 38, 39, 43 bottom left),
Tom DiPace (14), Goudey Gum Co. (16), Dell Publishing Co. (21),
Topps, Inc. (22, 28, 35 top left, 36, 40, 42 bottom), Turkey Red (34 bottom left),
Exhibit Supply Co. (34 bottom right), Macfadden Publications (41), Gum Inc. (42 top),
F.W. Rueckheim & Brother (45), Matt Richman (48).
Cover Photo: Michael Zagaris/Oakland Athletics/Getty Images

The memorabilia and artifacts pictured in this book are presented for educational and informational purposes,
and come from the collection of the author.

Editor: Mike Kennedy
Designer: Ron Jaffe
Project Management: Black Book Partners, LLC.
Special thanks to Topps, Inc.

Library of Congress Cataloging-in-Publication Data

Stewart, Mark, 1960-
  The Detroit Tigers / by Mark Stewart. -- Library ed.
    p. cm. -- (Team spirit)
  Includes bibliographical references and index.
  Summary: "A Team Spirit Baseball edition featuring the Detroit Tigers that
chronicles the history and accomplishments of the team. Includes access to
the Team Spirit website, which provides additional information, updates and
photos"--Provided by publisher.
  ISBN 978-1-59953-481-7 (library : alk. paper) -- ISBN 978-1-60357-361-0
(ebook) 1. Detroit Tigers (Baseball team)--History--Juvenile literature.
I. Title.
  GV875.D6S79 2012
  796.357'640977434--dc23
                                      2011048466

Manufactured in the United States of America in North Mankato, Minnesota.
196N—012012

COVER PHOTO: Pitcher and catcher meet on the mound to celebrate a Detroit victory in 2011.

TABLE OF CONTENTS

ABOUT OUR GLOSSARY

In this book, there may be several words that you are reading for the first time. Some are sports words, some are new vocabulary words, and some are familiar words that are used in an unusual way. All of these words are defined on page 46. Throughout the book, sports words appear in **bold type**. Regular vocabulary words appear in ***bold italic type***.

MEET THE TIGERS

Baseball fans love to trace the history of their game. The Detroit Tigers have been making history for more than 100 years. In fact, some of baseball's best hitters, fielders, and pitchers have worn the big *D* on their caps.

The Detroit players understand that they are links to the past. They respect the records and accomplishments of the old-timers. They also believe that, some day, future Tigers will look back at the example they have set. It is one of the reasons they give their best effort whenever they step on the field.

This book tells the story of the Tigers. They believe that a winning team starts with a winning attitude. Add some star players, a few hard-working teammates, plus a smart manager, and you have the recipe for a championship.

The Tigers congratulate Justin Verlander after a victory. He reminds many fans of old-time Detroit stars.

GLORY DAYS

COBB, DETROIT

I n 1901, the **American League (AL)** played its first season. Among the eight teams that made up the league were the Detroit Tigers. Fans in the city were very happy to have a new team. A club called the Detroit Wolverines had been champions in the **National League (NL)** during the 1800s, but they went out of business after the 1888 season. From 1894 to 1900, Detroit was home to a team in the **minor leagues**, but it just wasn't the same as watching **big-league** baseball.

The Tigers finished no higher than third until 1907. That year, Hughie Jennings became the manager, and Ty Cobb won his first of 11 batting championships. Jennings and Cobb were joined by Sam Crawford, the AL's top power hitter. The three helped Detroit win the **pennant** each year from 1907 to 1909.

The Tigers were fun to watch in their early years, but they did not win another pennant until the 1930s. That team was led by catcher

Mickey Cochrane, who was also the manager. His lineup starred some of the best hitters in history, including the "G-Men"—Hank Greenberg, Charlie Gehringer, and Goose Goslin. The Tigers captured the pennant in 1934 and 1935. They beat the Chicago Cubs in the 1935 **World Series** for their first championship.

The Tigers won the pennant again in 1940 and 1945. The 1945 club starred pitcher Hal Newhouser. He led the team to its second championship that fall.

During the 1950s, the Tigers found more young players for their lineup. Jim Bunning and Frank Lary were the stars of a strong **pitching staff**. Harvey Kuenn and Al Kaline helped form a dangerous batting order. Kaline went straight from high school to the big leagues and won

a batting championship when he was just 20 years old.

Kaline was still playing for the Tigers when they won their next championship, in 1968. Pitchers Denny McLain and Mickey Lolich led this team, but as always, Detroit had a lot of power in its lineup. Besides Kaline, the Tigers had sluggers Willie Horton, Norm Cash, and Jim Northrup. Detroit also had Bill Freehan, the AL's top catcher during the 1960s.

In 1984, the Tigers won the World Series again. This may have been Detroit's greatest team. The Tigers were in first place from the first day of the year until the last.

They were led by infielders Lou Whitaker and Alan Trammell, heavy hitters Lance Parrish and Kirk Gibson, and starting pitcher Jack Morris. Relief pitcher Willie Hernandez won the **Cy Young Award** and was named the league's **Most Valuable Player (MVP)**.

LEFT: Al Kaline   **ABOVE**: Willie Hernandez and Lance Parrish raise their arms in victory after the last out of the 1984 World Series.

Detroit manager Sparky Anderson was a master at getting the most out of his players. He knew whom to put in the lineup each game and when to make a change to energize his club. While the Tigers had many stars in 1984, they are best remembered for winning the championship with a total team effort.

Over the next 20 years, the Tigers tried to recapture the magic of the 1984 season. Many good players wore the Detroit uniform during this time, including Cecil Fielder, Travis Fryman, and Bobby Higginson. By 2003, however, the Tigers were barely **competitive**. That season they lost 119 games, more than any team in league history.

The news wasn't all bad for Tigers fans. The team had plenty of young talent—and more on the way in the minor leagues. In the years that followed, Curtis Granderson and Justin Verlander played their way into the starting lineup. By 2006, the team had added several **veterans**,

including Ivan Rodriguez, Magglio Ordonez, Placido Polanco, Kenny Rogers, and Todd Jones. They helped the Tigers win the **Wild Card** and reach the World Series.

The Tigers returned to the **playoffs** with a mostly new cast in 2011. Verlander had become the league's best pitcher. His new teammates included Miguel Cabrera, Victor Martinez, Alex Avila, Max Scherzer, Austin Jackson, and Jose Valverde. With players like these, Detroit fans expected to be in the playoff hunt almost every season.

LEFT: Justin Verlander   **ABOVE**: Miguel Cabrera

HOME TURF

For more than 80 years, the Tigers played in Tiger Stadium. The ballpark was called Navin Field when it opened in 1912. On the very same day, Fenway Park opened in Boston, Massachusetts. Neither story made the next morning's headlines. Instead, the country's newspapers reported the sinking of the ocean liner *Titanic*.

The Tigers moved into a new ballpark in 2000. One thing stayed the same—the team brought over home plate from Tiger Stadium. The ballpark's outfield fences are among the deepest in baseball. Because there is no upper deck in the outfield, fans have a wonderful view of the Detroit skyline. Under the stands, they can take a "walk through history" with a display that traces the story of life and baseball in Detroit since the 1800s.

BY THE NUMBERS

- *The Tigers' stadium has 41,255 seats.*
- *The distance from home plate to the left field foul pole is 345 feet.*
- *The distance from home plate to the center field fence is 420 feet.*
- *The distance from home plate to the right field foul pole is 330 feet.*

Tigers fans fill Detroit's stadium for a game during the 2007 season.

DRESSED FOR SUCCESS

The Tigers got their nickname during the 1890s, when they were still a minor-league team. They wore socks with yellow and black stripes, which reminded people of a tiger. In 1901, the Detroit players wore a cap with a tiger on the front. A few years later, the team started using an Old English-style *D* on their uniforms and caps.

Over the next 100 years, the Tigers tried many different uniform designs. Team colors included orange, black, red, white, and blue. In the mid-1990s, the Tigers switched to a uniform that reminded fans of the style worn by the championship teams of the 1930s and 1960s. Even when the Detroit uniform had a modern look, the ***traditional*** D was still used to keep a connection with the past.

LEFT: Victor Martinez hikes up the belt on his home uniform during a 2011 game.   **ABOVE**: George Kell signed this picture, which shows him in a road uniform from the 1950s.

WE WON!

The Tigers won four championships from 1935 to 1984. Each team was led by a group of great stars. The 1935 Tigers won the pennant thanks to veterans Charlie Gehringer, Mickey Cochrane, and Goose Goslin, plus the power hitting of young Hank Greenberg. Greenberg's wrist was broken by a pitch in the

Hank Greenberg

LITHO.IN U.S.A.

World Series, but the Detroit players pulled together and beat the Chicago Cubs four games to two. Pitcher Tommy Bridges won twice for the Tigers, and Goslin drove in the winning run in the bottom of the ninth inning of the final game.

Ten years later, the Tigers captured their second championship. Greenberg was now the veteran leader of the Tigers, and pitcher Hal Newhouser was the team's young star. Greenberg hit a **grand slam** on the final day of the 1945 season to win the pennant, and Newhouser led the AL in wins, strikeouts, and

LEFT: Hank Greenberg
RIGHT: Catcher Bill Freehan tags out Lou Brock in Game 5 of the 1968 World Series.

earned run average (ERA). Both were at their best in the World Series, again against the Cubs. The Tigers won four games to three.

The Tigers took their next pennant in 1968. This team was led by Denny McLain, who won 31 games. As usual, the Tigers had a lineup full of heavy hitters, including Al Kaline, Willie Horton, Bill Freehan, Norm Cash, and Jim Northrup. In all, eight different Tigers hit at least 10 home runs during the season. However, it was the pitching of Mickey Lolich that made the difference in the World Series against the St. Louis Cardinals. Lolich won Game 2, Game 5, and Game 7 to bring a third championship to Detroit.

Like the 1968 team, the 1984 Tigers were led by a group of talented and experienced players. Pitchers Jack Morris, Willie Hernandez, and Aurelio Lopez helped Detroit win 35 of their first 40

games. Lance Parrish was the team's catcher and most powerful hitter, while shortstop Alan Trammell and second baseman Lou Whitaker were baseball's best double-play partners. The heart of the team was Kirk Gibson. He energized his teammates game after game and put a charge into the crowd at home and on the road.

That year, the Tigers defeated the San Diego Padres in the World Series four games to one. Morris won two games, Hernandez saved Detroit's two other victories, and Trammell batted .450 for the series. Gibson made several good fielding plays against San Diego and was the hero in Game 5. With the score tied 3–3 in the fifth inning, he tagged up from third base and slid home safely on a pop fly to the second baseman. Three innings later, Gibson launched a home run into the upper deck to finish off the Padres and give the Tigers their fourth championship.

The Tigers nearly won their fifth championship in 2006. The team surprised the experts by making it to the

LEFT: Kirk Gibson waves to fans during the parade to celebrate the Tigers' 1984 championship.
RIGHT: Magglio Ordonez heads for home after his home run that won the pennant for Detroit in 2006.

playoffs just three seasons after losing a league-record 119 games. Pitching was Detroit's strength. Jeremy Bonderman, Justin Verlander, Nate Robertson, Kenny Rogers, Fernando Rodney, Joel Zumaya, and Todd Jones helped the Tigers build the league's best staff.

Detroit's excellent pitching continued against the New York Yankees and Oakland A's in the playoffs. The Tigers beat them both to win the pennant. Unfortunately, the Cardinals were the better team in the World Series. Detroit lost in five games. It was still a magical season that no Tigers fan will ever forget.

GO-TO GUYS

T o be a true star in baseball, you need more than a quick bat and a strong arm. You have to be a "go-to guy"—someone the manager wants on the pitcher's mound or in the batter's box when it matters most. Fans of the Tigers have had a lot to cheer about over the years, including these great stars …

 ## THE PIONEERS

TY COBB   Outfielder

• BORN: 12/18/1886   • DIED: 7/17/1961   • PLAYED FOR TEAM: 1905 TO 1926
Ty Cobb was a fierce and talented player who did whatever it took to win. He was disliked by opponents but also greatly respected. Cobb won 11 batting championships and retired with a .366 average—the highest in history.

HARRY HEILMANN   Outfielder

• BORN: 8/3/1894   • DIED: 7/9/1951   • PLAYED FOR TEAM: 1914 TO 1929
Harry Heilmann was Detroit's most dangerous hitter in the 1920s. He won four batting championships from 1921 to 1927. His best year came in 1923 when he hit .403.

CHARLIE GEHRINGER   Second Baseman

- BORN: 5/11/1903   • DIED: 1/21/1993   • PLAYED FOR TEAM: 1924 TO 1942

Charlie Gehringer was so smooth as a player and so quiet as a person that he was nicknamed the "Mechanical Man." He got more than 200 hits in a season seven times and won the batting championship in 1937.

HANK GREENBERG   First Baseman/Outfielder

- BORN: 1/1/1911   • DIED: 9/4/1986
- PLAYED FOR TEAM: 1930, 1933 TO 1941 & 1945 TO 1946

Hank Greenberg was one of the best right-handed sluggers in history. Due to injuries and time spent in the Army, he played only eight full seasons for the Tigers. He led the AL in home runs and **runs batted in (RBIs)** four times and was the MVP twice.

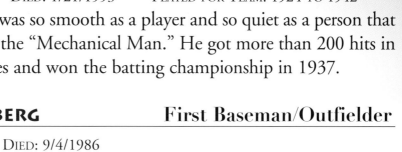

HAL NEWHOUSER   Pitcher

- BORN: 5/20/1921   • DIED: 11/10/1998
- PLAYED FOR TEAM: 1939 TO 1953

Hal Newhouser was an **All-Star** seven times during the 1940s. He used his blazing fastball to lead the AL in wins four times and strikeouts twice. From 1944 to 1946, Newhouser won 80 games for Detroit.

AL KALINE   Outfielder

- BORN: 12/19/1934   • PLAYED FOR TEAM: 1953 TO 1974

Al Kaline was often called the "perfect player." He was a very good hitter and a quick and graceful fielder. Kaline finished second in the AL MVP voting in 1955 and 1963.

ABOVE: Hal Newhouser

LOU WHITAKER Second Baseman

• BORN: 5/12/1957   • PLAYED FOR TEAM: 1977 TO 1995

Lou Whitaker was an excellent fielder and powerful hitter. He began his career in Detroit by being named the **Rookie of the Year**. Whitaker played together with Alan Trammell for 19 seasons—longer than any double-play combination in history.

ALAN TRAMMELL Shortstop

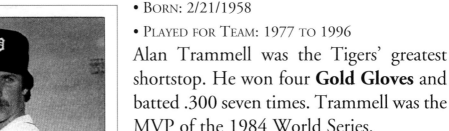

• BORN: 2/21/1958

• PLAYED FOR TEAM: 1977 TO 1996

Alan Trammell was the Tigers' greatest shortstop. He won four **Gold Gloves** and batted .300 seven times. Trammell was the MVP of the 1984 World Series.

JACK MORRIS Pitcher

• BORN: 5/16/1955

• PLAYED FOR TEAM: 1977 TO 1990

Jack Morris led the Tigers in wins each year from 1979 to 1988. He won more games than anyone in baseball during the 1980s and pitched two **complete games** in the 1984 World Series.

KIRK GIBSON   Outfielder

- BORN: 5/28/1957
- PLAYED FOR TEAM: 1979 TO 1987 & 1993 TO 1995

Kirk Gibson had amazing power, tremendous speed, and a talent for making great plays when the Tigers needed them most. He led the team in stolen bases four years in a row.

JUSTIN VERLANDER   Pitcher

- BORN: 2/20/1983
- FIRST YEAR WITH TEAM: 2005

At the age of 28, most pitchers are just beginning to have success in the big leagues. By his 28th birthday, Justin Verlander had pitched two **no-hitters**, won his 100th game, and struck out his 1,000th batter. In 2011, he led the AL in wins, strikeouts, and ERA.

MIGUEL CABRERA   First Baseman

- BORN: 4/18/1983   • FIRST YEAR WITH TEAM: 2008

One of the best trades Detroit ever made was the one for Miguel Cabrera. He was the AL home run leader in his first year with the Tigers. In 2011, Cabrera hit .344 to win the league batting championship.

LEFT: Jack Morris   **ABOVE**: After his playing days, Kirk Gibson returned to coach the Tigers.

During more than a century of baseball, the Tigers have had some of the game's most famous and talented managers. Mickey Cochrane, Ty Cobb, and Alan Trammell all starred as players for Detroit and later managed the team. Another great player who led the Tigers was Hughie Jennings. He was a star in the 1800s. Jennings guided the Tigers to the pennant each year from 1907 to 1909. Other managers who won pennants in Detroit include Del Baker, Steve O'Neill, and Mayo Smith.

JENNINGS, DETROIT

In 1979, the Tigers hired Sparky Anderson to manage the team. He had already won four pennants and two World Series with the Cincinnati Reds in the NL. Anderson was a good teacher who helped Detroit's young players gain confidence. He made sure to put them in situations where they had the best chance to succeed. That is what a great manager does.

In 1984, Anderson put all of the pieces together and guided the Tigers to their fourth World Series championship. That team was unstoppable. Detroit won 104 games during the regular season and then lost just once in the playoffs.

Jim Leyland was often compared to Anderson. Before he joined the Tigers in 2006, he had turned two so-so teams—the Pittsburgh Pirates and Florida Marlins—into winners. With Detroit, Leyland demanded two things from his players. He asked that they always be prepared and that they always give their best effort. The players worked extra-hard to please their new manager. In Leyland's first six seasons, the Tigers made the playoffs twice and won the pennant once.

ONE GREAT DAY

When the Tigers and St. Louis Cardinals met in Game 7 of the 1968 World Series, not many people thought Detroit had a chance. The Cardinals handed the ball to Bob Gibson, baseball's best pitcher. He had already beaten the Tigers twice, allowing only one run in 18 innings. In Game 1, he set a record by striking out 17 Detroit batters.

The only man standing between the Cardinals and the championship was Mickey Lolich—and it was a miracle that he was even standing. As a boy, he was in a motorcycle accident. During his recovery, he noticed that his left arm had become much stronger than his right arm. Even though he was born right-handed, he began pitching left-handed.

Lolich had already beaten the Cardinals in Game 2 and Game 5. Detroit manager Mayo Smith asked him to start Game 7 on just two days of rest. Lolich and Gibson battled each other inning after inning. Neither team could move a runner past first base, and both teams made excellent fielding plays. Lou Brock and Curt Flood

The Tigers lift Mickey Lolich off the ground after his victory in Game 7.

each reached first base in the sixth inning, and both planned to steal second. Lolich picked them off before they had the chance.

The Tigers and Cardinals began the seventh inning in a 0–0 tie. With two outs, Norm Cash and Willie Horton hit singles. The next batter, Jim Northrup, lined a ball to deep center field off Gibson. Flood misjudged the ball for an instant and could not get back in time to catch it. Two runs scored, and the Tigers went on to win 4–1.

Most baseball fans knew very little about Lolich before the World Series—but that soon changed. His name was in newspaper headlines all over the country. "All of my life, somebody has been the big star and Mickey Lolich was the number-two guy," he said after Game 7. "I figured my day would come, and this was it."

LEGEND HAS IT

TIGERS

BILL FREEHAN   catcher

WHICH TIGER HAD THE STRICTEST FATHER?

LEGEND HAS IT that Bill Freehan did. Freehan was a baseball and football star in college during the early 1960s. The Tigers gave him $125,000 to leave school and join their team. Since Freehan was under 21, he needed his father's permission. He agreed, but only if his son promised to finish college. Freehan's father would not allow him to spend a nickel of the money until he made good on his promise. In 1966, Freehan finally finished his schoolwork and got his diploma. By that time, he was already an All-Star catcher and Gold Glove winner for Detroit.

WHO WAS THE FIRST PITCHER TO WATCH VIDEO OF HIMSELF?

LEGEND HAS IT that Hal Newhouser was. Newhouser was tall and skinny. To control his fastball and curveball, his pitching motion had to be perfect. During the 1940s, Newhouser started watching movies of himself between starts to see if he was making mistakes. He compared old films to ones from recent games that were shot with a powerful lens. The tiny differences he noticed helped him correct his flaws. Today, all teams have their pitchers study video of themselves.

WHICH DETROIT PITCHER TALKED TO BASEBALLS ON THE MOUND?

LEGEND HAS IT that Mark Fidrych did. Fidrych looked more like a Little Leaguer than a big leaguer when he pitched for the Tigers in 1976. The rookie not only talked to the baseball, he jumped for joy after outs and shook hands with his infielders after good plays. Before each inning, Fidrych would drop to his knees and rearrange the dirt on the mound. Detroit fans adored Fidrych and nicknamed him "The Bird." Almost a million people came to watch his 29 starts in 1976.

Close plays at first base are among the most difficult for umpires to call. Fans often boo when they believe an ump has made a bad decision, even if the replay shows that he got it right. Once in a great while, the umpire makes the wrong call at first base. This is just part of baseball. Nobody's perfect, right?

Well, in June of 2010, Armando Galarraga was as close to perfect as a pitcher can be. Through eight innings, not a single batter for the Cleveland Indians had reached first base safely. Galarraga retired the first two hitters in the ninth inning. With one more out, he would have the first **perfect game** in team history.

Galarraga delivered a pitch to Jason Donald, who tapped a slow grounder to Miguel Cabrera near first base. Galarraga raced to the bag to receive Cabrera's throw. The ball bounced around in Galarraga's glove for a moment as he touched first base. Then Donald crossed the bag. To umpire Jim Joyce, it looked as if Galarraga did not have control of the ball. Joyce called the runner safe. Galarraga got the final out moments later for a 3–0 victory. But he had lost his perfect game.

Armando Galarraga works on his fielding during a practice in 2010. He did everything right against the Cleveland Indians later that season.

Afterward, Detroit fans were furious. To their surprise, Galarraga was not angry. Instead, he was happy because he had pitched his best game ever, and the Tigers had won. He said that Joyce probably felt worse than he did. Galarraga was right—Joyce knew he had missed the call and was in tears after the game.

Just before the next day's game, Galarraga brought Detroit's lineup card to home plate and handed it to Joyce. They shook hands, and Joyce gave Galaragga a grateful pat on the back. Later, the two wrote a book together. Its title? *Nobody's Perfect.*

TEAM SPIRIT

When Detroit fans roar, their stadium sounds like the world's biggest wild animal park. They are loud and proud and loyal. When the Tigers win, there is no ballpark in baseball with more energy. When the team loses, the fans look at each other and think, *We'll get 'em next time.* That is one of the reasons that players often spend 10 years  or more with the Tigers. They love playing for the crowds in Detroit.

No one loved Tigers fans more than broadcasters Ernie Harwell and George Kell. The fans loved them right back. People in Detroit spent countless hours listening to Harwell and Kell call Tigers games on television and radio. The pair made it into the **Hall of Fame**—Harwell as an announcer and Kell as a player.

LEFT: Detroit fans like to show their "stripes" at Detroit's ballpark.
ABOVE: The fans at Tiger Stadium show their support during the 1960s.

TIMELINE

Members of the 1935 Tigers pose in the dugout before a World Series game.

1901

The Tigers finish third in their first season.

1935

The Tigers win their first championship.

1907

Ty Cobb leads the Tigers to their first pennant.

1943

Dick Wakefield leads the AL with 200 hits.

1949

George Kell leads the AL in batting.

Ty Cobb

George Kell

'74 Highlights

KALINE JOINS 3000 HIT CLUB

Al Kaline

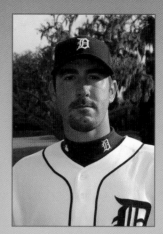

Justin Verlander

1974
Al Kaline gets his 3,000th hit.

1984
The Tigers win their fourth championship.

2011
Justin Verlander wins the Cy Young Award and the MVP.

1968
The Tigers win their third championship.

2006
The Tigers win the pennant for the first time since 1984.

Magglio Ordonez led the 2006 Tigers with 104 RBIs.

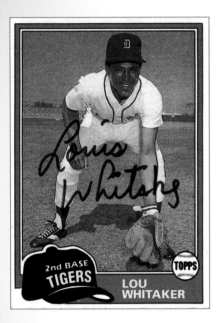

Fab Four

In 1986, all four members of the Tigers' infield—first baseman Darrell Evans, second baseman Lou Whitaker, shortstop Alan Trammell, and third baseman Darnell Coles—hit 20 or more home runs.

One & Done

In his first game as a Tiger, 19-year-old pitcher Denny McLain hit a home run against the Chicago White Sox. McLain would go on to win two Cy Young Awards in his career. But he never hit another home run.

Pitching Politics

Jim Bunning was Detroit's top pitcher during the 1950s. He led the AL in strikeouts twice and pitched a no-hitter in 1958. After leaving baseball, Bunning became a U.S. Senator.

RUDY! RUDY!

Rudy York had the greatest month of any baseball rookie in 1937. That August, he hit 18 home runs and drove in 49 runs. Both are still AL records.

POSITION SWITCH

In 2004, the Tigers decided that catcher Brandon Inge did not have the skills to play catcher every day in the big leagues. They asked him to try third base. Within a year, Inge was one of baseball's best-fielding third basemen.

A MATTER OF PRIDE

In 1996, the Tigers signed Curtis Pride, a hearing-impaired outfielder. Pride could not hear the sounds of the game, but he could feel the roar of the crowd in his chest after he got a hit. Pride played in 95 games that season and batted .300—the second highest average on the team.

LEFT: Lou Whitaker   **ABOVE**: Brandon Inge makes a play at third base.

TALKING BASEBALL

"I'm doing what I love to do most. How can I feel pressure doing what I love to do?"

► **MIGUEL CABRERA**, ON WHY HE IS SO RELAXED DURING GAMES

"I'm hoping to learn something new every day. It sounds corny, but I really do come in here every day, listening and talking with the veteran guys and seeing what I can absorb."

► **JUSTIN VERLANDER**, ON BEING A STUDENT OF THE GAME

"I couldn't wait to get to the ballpark. I'd be the first one there and I was willing to do anything. I think that's why the veterans liked me."

► **AL KALINE**, ON HOW HE FIT IN WITH THE OLDER TIGERS AS A TEENAGER

"George was a friend to many people. What a super man."

▶ **ALAN TRAMMELL**, *ON LONGTIME TIGERS PLAYER AND BROADCASTER GEORGE KELL*

"I never could stand losing. Second place didn't interest me."

▶ **TY COBB**, *ON HIS DESIRE TO WIN*

"Baseball is a simple game. If you have good players and if you keep them in the right frame of mind, then the manager is a success."

▶ **SPARKY ANDERSON**, *ON WHAT MAKES A GOOD MANAGER*

"When you're playing, awards don't seem like much. Then you get older and all of it becomes more precious. It is nice to be remembered."

▶ **HANK GREENBERG**, *ON HIS TWO MVP AWARDS*

LEFT: Miguel Cabrera   **ABOVE**: Alan Trammell

GREAT DEBATES

eople who root for the Tigers love to compare their favorite moments, teams, and players. Some debates have been going on for years! How would you settle these classic baseball arguments?

DENNY MCLAIN HAD THE FINEST YEAR OF ANY DETROIT PITCHER IN 1968 ...

... because he was the first player in a *generation* to win 30 games. McLain (LEFT) went 31–6 with a 1.96 ERA and six **shutouts**. He pitched more innings and faced more batters than anyone in the league. He might have finished with 33 wins, except the Tigers lost his last two games, both 2–1.

HELLO! JUSTIN VERLANDER HAD A MUCH BETTER SEASON IN 2011 ...

... because he went 24–5 in only 34 starts and pitched a no-hitter. In fact, Verlander almost had three no-hitters—he came close in June and again in July. Like McLain, Verlander was the AL's top winner and pitched the most innings. But he also had the league's lowest ERA and the most strikeouts.

AL KALINE WAS THE TIGERS' GREATEST ALL-AROUND PLAYER ...

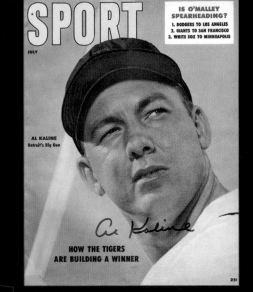

... because he won games with his bat and his glove. Kaline (RIGHT) captured a batting championship at the age of 20 and was still hitting .300 at age 37. He was the best right fielder in baseball in the 1950s and 1960s. Kaline won the Gold Glove 10 out of the first 11 years they gave out the award. He also had a great arm. When he had the ball, baserunners stopped dead in their tracks. Kaline finished in the Top 10 in the AL MVP voting nine times.

SERIOUSLY? MOST FANS WOULDN'T TRADE TY COBB FOR THREE AL KALINES ...

... because Cobb would stop at nothing to win games. He played every inning like his life depended on it. Opponents were terrified of getting in his way. So were teammates! Cobb had more than 4,000 hits. He had the highest lifetime average of any player. He won 11 batting titles. Cobb also led the league in RBIs four times, runs scored five times, and stolen bases six times. Kaline was a nicer guy, but no one was a fiercer competitor than Cobb.

The great Tigers teams and players have left their marks on the record books. These are the "best of the best" …

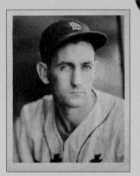

Charlie Gehringer

Harvey Kuenn

TIGERS AWARD WINNERS

WINNER	AWARD	YEAR
Mickey Cochrane	Most Valuable Player	1934
Hank Greenberg	Most Valuable Player	1935
Charlie Gehringer	Most Valuable Player	1937
Hank Greenberg	Most Valuable Player	1940
Hal Newhouser	Most Valuable Player	1944
Hal Newhouser	Most Valuable Player	1945
Harvey Kuenn	Rookie of the Year	1953
Denny McLain	Cy Young Award	1968
Denny McLain	Most Valuable Player	1968
Mickey Lolich	World Series MVP	1968
Denny McLain	Cy Young Award	1969
Mark Fidrych	Rookie of the Year	1976
Lou Whitaker	Rookie of the Year	1978
Sparky Anderson	Manager of the Year	1984
Willie Hernandez	Cy Young Award	1984
Willie Hernandez	Most Valuable Player	1984
Alan Trammell	World Series MVP	1984
Sparky Anderson	Manager of the Year	1987
Justin Verlander	Rookie of the Year	2006
Jim Leyland	Manager of the Year	2006
Justin Verlander	Cy Young Award	2011
Justin Verlander	Most Valuable Player	2011

ACHIEVEMENT	YEAR
AL Pennant Winner	1907
AL Pennant Winner	1908
AL Pennant Winner	1909
AL Pennant Winner	1934
AL Pennant Winner	1935
World Series Champions	1935
AL Pennant Winner	1940
AL Pennant Winner	1945
World Series Champions	1945
AL Pennant Winner	1968
World Series Champions	1968
AL East Champions	1972
AL East Champions	1984
AL Pennant Winner	1984
World Series Champions	1984
AL East Champions	1987
AL Wild Card Winner	2006
AL Pennant Winner	2006
AL Central Champions	2011

ABOVE: Mark Fidrych
LEFT: Jim Leyland

PINPOINTS

The history of a baseball team is made up of many smaller stories. These stories take place all over the map—not just in the city a team calls "home." Match the pushpins on these maps to the **TEAM FACTS**, and you will begin to see the story of the Tigers unfold!

TEAM FACTS

1. Detroit, Michigan—*The team has played here since 1901.*
2. St. Paul, Minnesota—*Jack Morris was born here.*
3. New York, New York—*Hank Greenberg was born here.*
4. Narrows, Georgia—*Ty Cobb was born here.*
5. Chicago, Illinois—*The Tigers won the 1945 World Series here.*
6. St. Louis, Missouri—*The Tigers won the 1968 World Series here.*
7. Wahoo, Nebraska—*Sam Crawford was born here.*
8. Portland, Oregon—*Mickey Lolich was born here.*
9. San Francisco, California—*Harry Heilmann was born here.*
10. Tecamachalco, Mexico—*Aurelio Lopez was born here.*
11. Bolivar, Venezuela—*Victor Martinez was born here.*
12. Aguada, Puerto Rico—*Willie Hernandez was born here.*

CRAWFORD, Detroit - Americans

Sam Crawford

GLOSSARY

ALL-STAR—A player who is selected to play in baseball's annual All-Star Game.

AMERICAN LEAGUE (AL)—One of baseball's two major leagues; the AL began play in 1901.

BIG-LEAGUE—The top level of professional baseball, also called major-league.

COMPETITIVE—Having the ability and desire to win.

COMPLETE GAMES—Games started and finished by the same pitcher.

CY YOUNG AWARD—The award given each year to each league's best pitcher.

EARNED RUN AVERAGE (ERA)—A statistic that measures how many runs a pitcher gives up for every nine innings he pitches.

GENERATION—A period of years roughly equal to the time it takes for a person to be born, grow up, and have children.

GOLD GLOVES—The awards given each year to baseball's best fielders.

GRAND SLAM—A home run with the bases loaded.

HALL OF FAME—The museum in Cooperstown, New York, where baseball's greatest players are honored.

MINOR LEAGUES—The many professional leagues that help develop players for the major leagues.

MOST VALUABLE PLAYER (MVP)—The award given each year to each league's top player; an MVP is also selected for the World Series and the All-Star Game.

NATIONAL LEAGUE (NL)—The older of the two major leagues; the NL began play in 1876.

NO-HITTERS—Games in which a team does not get a hit.

PENNANT—A league championship. The term comes from the triangular flag awarded to each season's champion, beginning in the 1870s.

PERFECT GAME—A game in which no batter reaches base.

PITCHING STAFF—The group of players who pitch for a team.

PLAYOFFS—The games played after the regular season to determine which teams will advance to the World Series.

ROOKIE OF THE YEAR—The annual award given to each league's best first-year player.

RUNS BATTED IN (RBIs)—A statistic that counts the number of runners a batter drives home.

SHUTOUTS—Games in which one team does not score a run.

TRADITIONAL—Done the same way from generation to generation.

VETERANS—Players with great experience.

WILD CARD—A playoff spot reserved for a team that does not win its division, but finishes with a good record.

WORLD SERIES—The world championship series played between the AL and NL pennant winners.

EXTRA INNINGS

TEAM SPIRIT introduces a great way to stay up to date with your team! Visit our **EXTRA INNINGS** link and get connected to the latest and greatest updates. **EXTRA INNINGS** serves as a young reader's ticket to an exclusive web page—with more stories, fun facts, team records, and photos of the Tigers. Content is updated during and after each season. The **EXTRA INNINGS** feature also enables readers to send comments and letters to the author! Log onto:

www.norwoodhousepress.com/library.aspx

and click on the tab: **TEAM SPIRIT** to access **EXTRA INNINGS**.

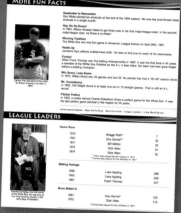

Read all the books in the series to learn more about professional sports. For a complete listing of the baseball, basketball, football, and hockey teams in the **TEAM SPIRIT** series, visit our website at:

www.norwoodhousepress.com/library.aspx

ON THE ROAD

DETROIT TIGERS
2100 Woodward Avenue
Detroit, Michigan 48201
(313) 471-2000
detroit.tigers.mlb.com

**NATIONAL BASEBALL
HALL OF FAME AND MUSEUM**
25 Main Street
Cooperstown, New York 13326
(888) 425-5633
www.baseballhalloffame.org

ON THE BOOKSHELF

To learn more about the sport of baseball, look for these books at your library or bookstore:

- Augustyn, Adam (editor). *The Britannica Guide to Baseball*. New York, NY: Rosen Publishing, 2011.

- Dreier, David. *Baseball: How It Works*. North Mankato, MN: Capstone Press, 2010.

- Stewart, Mark. *Ultimate 10: Baseball*. New York, NY: Gareth Stevens Publishing, 2009.

INDEX

PAGE NUMBERS IN **BOLD** REFER TO ILLUSTRATIONS.

ABOUT THE AUTHOR

MARK STEWART has written more than 50 books on baseball and over 150 sports books for kids. He grew up in New York City during the 1960s rooting for the Yankees and Mets, and was lucky enough to meet players from both teams. Mark comes from a family of writers. His grandfather was Sunday Editor of *The New York Times,* and his mother was Articles Editor of *Ladies' Home Journal* and *McCall's.* Mark has profiled hundreds of athletes over the past 25 years. He has also written several books about his native New York and New Jersey, his home today. Mark is a graduate of Duke University, with a degree in history. He lives and works in a home overlooking Sandy Hook, New Jersey. You can contact Mark through the Norwood House Press website.